Quick Hangeul
How to Read Korean Alphabet in One Hour!

Written by   Heechul Cho
Publisher   Kyudo Chung
Published by   Darakwon

First Published   2025. 3. 20

Editorial Planner   Hyukju Kwon, Taekwang Kim
Editor   Huchun Lee, Hyoeun Kim, Soyoung Park

Designed by   SINGTA Design
Image   iclickart, shutterstock

🐊 DARAKWON

Darakwon Bldg., 211 Munbal-ro, Paju-si, Gyeonggi-do, Republic of Korea 10881
Tel : 02-736-2031
Fax : 02-732-2037
(Marketing Dept. ext.:250~252, Editorial Dept. ext.: 291~296)

ISBN 978-89-277-7483-9   13710

http://www.darakwon.co.kr
http://www.darakwonusa.com

Visit the Darakwon homepage to learn about our other publications and promotions and to download the contents in MP3 format.

한글  마스터 하기!

Quick HANGEUL

Master **Korean Alphabet**
Through Visual Examples

Written by **Heechul Cho**

How to Read Korean Alphabet
in ONE HOUR!

🔲 **DARAKWON**

Preface

The Korean alphabet, Hangeul, is the first step to learning the Korean language. The challenge of learning Hangeul is in the number of characters and it's unique trait, which allows new characters to be created by combining existing characters. Hence, learning Hangeul is more difficult than people commonly think.

I have been teaching Korean to university students and the general public in Japan for quite some time, and I understand very well how difficult it is to learn Hangeul. There are countless cases where people cannot read Korean correctly even after studying Hangeul for months, so I developed a new way to memorize Hangeul with images.

Many Westerners who learn Korean perceive Hangeul as similar to pictographs. The mnemonic proposed in this book is based on the concept of Hangeul's pictorial appearance. This book is the English version of "A Textbook to Read Hangeul in One Hour," which was published in Japan in 2011 and has sold over 800,000 copies (including similar books) to date, receiving overwhelming support from readers.

Naturally, this book is designed to make it easy for
native English speakers to learn Hangeul. I hope that everyone
who picks up this book will have fun and learn Hangeul easily.

I would like to thank Dain Kim for giving me many ideas and
for publishing this book, Jihye Kim and Lisandra Moor for
checking the English expressions, and Huchun Lee of Publisher
Darakwon Publishing.

Heechul Cho

A comprehensive introduction to the Korean Alphabet!

This book focuses on learning Hangeul so you can read and write with confidence!

Vowels & Consonants

You can learn shapes and sounds of consonants and vowels. Try writing the hangeul in the correct stroke order and practice the pronunciation. And you'll discover a wide vocabulary through the letters you've learned.

Visual Examples

A variety of visual examples are provided to show how each letter is used. You'll also learn useful Korean words.

Audio files

You can learn the correct pronunciation of each word by listening to native Korean speakers. As you listen and read multiple times, you'll naturally become familiar with Korean pronunciation.

FREE
Audio files

www.
darakwonusa.
com

Review

Each chapter includes writing practice to review words you've learned.

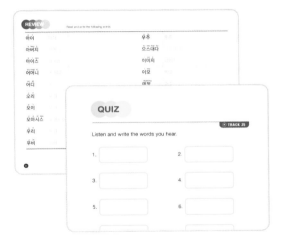

Appendix

The [Appendix] includes various styles of Hangeul letters, helping you become familiar with their characteristics. Additionally, learners can practice reading and writing basic Korean expressions.

Table of Contents

PART 1
Korean Vowels

1 **The Different Types of Simple Vowels(eight vowels)**

아 어 오 우 으 이 애 에

2 **The "Y" Group Vowels**

야 여 요 유 얘 예

3 **The "W" Group Vowels**

와 왜 외 워 웨 위

4 **The Diphthongs Vowel**

의

PART 2
Korean Consonants

PART 1
ㅣ
Korean
Vowels

Vowels of Hangeul are created by combining '·, —, |.' The combination of these three characters creates a multiplicity of vowels.

For example, adding '·' to the right of ' | ' makes ' ㅏ [a]' and adding '·' on top of '—[eu]' makes 'ㅗ[o].'

| + • = ㅏ *a*

• + — = ㅗ *o*

Adding '·' to the left of ' | ' makes ' ㅓ [eo]' and adding '·' under '—' makes 'ㅜ[u].'

• + | = ㅓ *eo*

— + • = ㅜ *u*

Adding another '·' to the above-mentioned vowels gives us 'ㅑ [ya]/ㅛ[yo]' and 'ㅕ [yeo]/ㅠ[yu],' respectively.

The Korean vowels that can be made with this combination are as follows. The consonant "ㅇ" will act as a silent placeholder.

아	야	어	여	오			요	우			유	으	이
애	얘	에	예	와	왜	외		워	웨	위		의	

The Different Types of Simple Vowels (eight vowels)

Korean vowels are consisted of 10 simple vowels and 11 complex vowels. Based on pronunciation, however, there is a total of 8 simple vowels in addition to the 13 complex vowels created by synthesizing the aforementioned simple vowels.

Simple vowels refer to a set of vowels that do not require a change the position of the tongue or the shape of the lips — otherwise known as a speaker's articulators. On the contrary, complex vowels are those by which the position of the tongue or the shape of the lips changes upon pronunciation.

From now on, we will examine the simple vowels.

The followings are the eight simple vowels.

Let's learn about the sounds and shapes of the vowels, and the words they are used in.

ㅏ (아) sounds like <u>a</u> in f<u>a</u>ther

f ㅏ ther

ㅏ = 아 → a

▶ TRACK 02

아 이 child

아 버 지 father

아 이 스 ice

Find the letters 아 in the images below.

아메리카노

아빠

아이스크림

ㅓ (어) sounds like *eo* in father

fath **ㅓ** r

ㅓ = 어 → eo

▶ TRACK 03

어

^{eo} ^{meo} ⁿⁱ
어 머 니 mother

^{eo} ^{bu}
어 부 fisherman

^{eo} ^{di}
어 디 where

ㅓ

Find the letters **어** in the images below.

어워드

아이디어

어린이날

ㅗ(오) sounds like _o_ in _door_

d ㅗ r

$$ㅗ = 오 → O$$

▶ TRACK 04

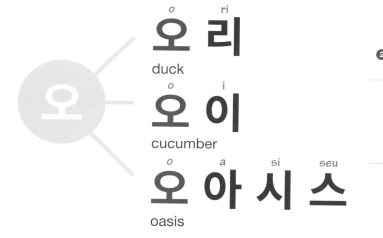

오

오 리
duck

오 이
cucumber

오 아 시 스
oasis

Find the letters 오 in the images below.

오늘

오래오래

오리

아 어 **오** 우 으 이 애 에

ㅜ(우) sounds like <u>u</u> in <i>food</i>

f ㅜ d

ㅜ = 우 → u

▶ TRACK 05

우리 _{we}
^u ^{ri}

우비 _{raincoat}
^u ^{bi}

우주 _{universe}
^u ^{ju}

Find the letters 우 in the images below.

우리 한우

우유

우동

아 어 오 **우** 으 이 애 에

ㅡ(으) sounds like *eu* in sky

s — ky

$$ \boxed{\quad} = 으 \rightarrow eu $$

ㅡ(으) sounds like between the letter "s" and "ky" in the word "sky." There is no equivalent vowel in the English language. When you pronounce '으', pull your lips back and make sure your lips aren't protruding outward.

▶ TRACK 06

eu *seu* *dae* *da*
으 스 대 다
show off

eu *ri* *eu* *ri* *ha* *da*
으 리 으 리 하 다
magnificent

① →

Find the letters 으 in the images below.

으뜸

"으쓱"

으쓱

"으라차차"

으라차차

아 어 오 우 **으** 이 애 에

ㅣ (이) sounds like i̱ in kiss

k ㅣ ss

$$ㅣ = 이 \rightarrow i$$

▶ TRACK 07

이 ⟨

i ri
이 리 wolf

i mi ji
이 미 지 image

i mo
이 모 aunt

ㅣ ❶

Find the letters **이** in the images below.

마이, 라이프

이사

이천

ㅐ (애) sounds like _ae_ in _apple_

애 pple

ㅐ = 애 → ae

▶ TRACK 08

애 _ae_ 정 _jeong_ love

애 _ae_ 교 _gyo_ charms

애 _ae_ 수 _su_ sorrow

Find the letters **애** in the images below.

연애

애견

애그플레이션

아 어 오 우 으 이 **애** 에

ㅔ (에) sounds like *e* in *error*

에 rror

ㅔ = 에 → e

에 어 컨
e *eo* *keon*
airconditioner

에 너 지
e *neo* *ji*
energy

에 이 스
e *i* *seu*
ace

Find the letters 에 in the images below.

무이네에서

에너지

크리에이터

Read and write the following words.

a i **아이**	아이		
a beo ji **아버지**	아버지		
a i seu **아이스**	아이스		
eo meo ni **어머니**	어머니		
eo di **어디**	어디		
o ri **오리**	오리		
o i **오이**	오이		
o a si seu **오아시스**	오아시스		
u ri **우리**	우리		
u bi **우비**	우비		

우주 u ju	우주		
으스대다 eu seu dae da	으스대다		
이미지 i mi ji	이미지		
이모 i mo	이모		
애정 ae jeong	애정		
애교 ae gyo	애교		
애수 ae su	애수		
에어컨 e eo keon	에어컨		
에너지 e neo ji	에너지		
에이스 e i seu	에이스		

The "Y" Group Vowels

There is a total of 6 "Y" group vowels. They are created by adding short horizontal or vertical stroke to the 6 vowels — 아[a], 어[eo], 오[o], 우[u], 애[ae], 에[e] — with the exception of '으/이.'

Combination	Example
ᅡ a + • = ᅣ ya	야 갸 냐 먀 샤
ᅥ eo + • = ᅧ yeo	여 겨 녀 며 셔
ᅩ o + • = ᅭ yo	요 교 뇨 묘 쇼
ᅮ u + • = ᅲ yu	유 규 뉴 뮤 슈
ᅢ ae + • = ᅤ yae	얘 걔 쟤
ᅦ e + • = ᅨ ye	예 계 례 폐 혜

▶ The consonant ㅇ will act as a silent placeholder.

ㅑ (야) sounds like <u>ya</u> in shout

sh ㅑ ut

from

▶ TRACK 11

ya
ㅑ

○ + ㅑ (ya) = 야 (ya)		
ㄱ (g) + ㅑ (ya) = 가 (gya)		
ㄴ (n) + ㅑ (ya) = 냐 (nya)		
ㅁ (m) + ㅑ (ya) = 먀 (mya)		
ㅅ (s) + ㅑ (ya) = 샤 (sya)		

야 _{ya} 구 _{gu} baseball

샤 _{sya} 워 _{weo} shower

에 _e 스 _{seu} 파 _{pa} 냐 _{nya} Espana

Find the letters 'consonant + ㅑ' in the images below.

심야

샤워

에스파냐

ㅕ (여) sounds like <u>yeo</u> in y<u>u</u>mmy

여 mmy

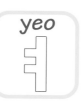
yeo from eo

▶ TRACK 12

yeo

○	+	ㅕ yeo	=	여 yeo	
ㄱ g	+	ㅕ yeo	=	겨 gyeo	
ㄴ n	+	ㅕ yeo	=	녀 nyeo	
ㅁ m	+	ㅕ yeo	=	며 myeo	
ㅅ s	+	ㅕ yeo	=	셔 syeo	

30

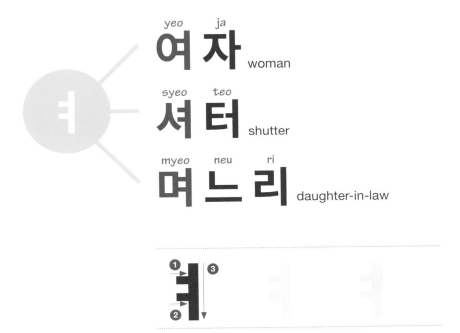

여 *yeo* 자 *ja* woman

셔 *syeo* 터 *teo* shutter

며 *myeo* 느 *neu* 리 *ri* daughter-in-law

Find the letters 'consonant + ㅕ' in the images below.

겨울

해녀

여름

ㅛ(ㅛ) sounds like _yo_ in _yoga_

ㅛ ga

yo from o

▶ TRACK 13

yo

◯ + ㅛ = ㅛ
    yo   yo

ㄱ + ㅛ = ㅛ
g   yo   gyo

ㄴ + ㅛ = ㅛ
n   yo   nyo

ㅁ + ㅛ = ㅛ
m   yo   myo

ㅅ + ㅛ = ㅛ
s   yo   syo

요 리 ^{yo ri} cooking

묘 사 ^{myo sa} description

쇼 트 케 이 크 ^{syo teu ke i keu} shortcake

ㅛ

Find the letters 'consonant + ㅛ' in the images below.

쇼핑

교실

애묘

ㅠ(유) sounds like yu in you

유

 from

yu   u

▶ TRACK 14

yu

ㅠ

○ + ㅠ = 유
    yu   yu

ㄱ + ㅠ = 규
g   yu   gyu

ㄴ + ㅠ = 뉴
n   yu   nyu

ㅁ + ㅠ = 뮤
m   yu   myu

ㅅ + ㅠ = 슈
s   yu   syu

34

유 리 glass
yu *ri*

규 모 scale
gyu *mo*

뉴 스 news
nyu *seu*

Find the letters 'consonant + ㅠ' in the images below.

뉴욕

슈

유기농

ㅒ (얘) sounds like yea in yeah

yae

from

ae ㅐ

▶ TRACK 15

yae ㅒ

○ + ㅒ(yae) = 애(yae)

ㄱ(g) + ㅒ(yae) = 걔(gyae)

ㅅ(s) + ㅒ(yae) = 섀(syae)

ㅈ(j) + ㅒ(yae) = 쟤(jyae)

얘 기 story
yae *gi*

섀 도 shadow
syae *do*

하 얘 요 white
ha *yae* *yo*

Find the letters 'consonant + ㅒ' in the images below.

아이섀도

얘들

하얘요

ㅖ (예) sounds like _ye_ in _yes_

예 s

_ye_ ㅖ from _e_ ㅔ

▶ TRACK 16

_ye_ ㅖ

○	+	ㅖ _ye_	= 예 _ye_
ㄱ _g_	+	ㅖ _ye_	= 계 _gye_
ㄹ _r_	+	ㅖ _ye_	= 례 _rye_
ㅅ _s_	+	ㅖ _ye_	= 셰 _sye_
ㅍ _p_	+	ㅖ _ye_	= 폐 _pye_

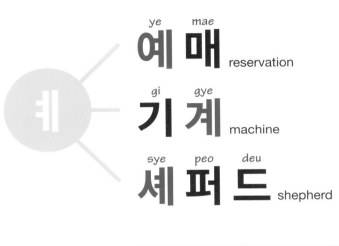

ye *mae*
예 매 reservation

gi *gye*
기 계 machine

sye *peo* *deu*
셰 퍼 드 shepherd

Find the letters 'consonant + ㅖ' in the images below.

세계

계절

예산, 수혜자

Read and write the following words.

ya gu 야구	야구		
sya weo 샤워	샤워		
e seu pa nya 에스파냐	에스파냐		
yeo ja 여자	여자		
sheo teo 셔터	셔터		
myeo neu ri 며느리	며느리		
yo ri 요리	요리		
myo sa 묘사	묘사		
sho teu ke i keu 쇼트케이크	쇼트케이크		

yu ri 유리	유리		
gyu mo 규모	규모		
nyu seu 뉴스	뉴스		
yae gi 얘기	얘기		
syae do 섀도	섀도		
ha yae yo 하얘요	하얘요		
ye mae 예매	예매		
gi gye 기계	기계		
sye peo deu 셰퍼드	셰퍼드		

The "W" Group Vowels

There are certain vowels created by merging 'o[ㅗ]' or 'u[ㅜ]' to other existing vowels. The vowels are double vowels. Because these are double vowels, when pronouncing them think of the letter "w" and pronounce them as you would pronounce words that begin "w."

1. Vowels created by adding other vowels to ㅗ°

Combination	Example
ㅗ°→w **+** ㅏ^a = ㅘ^{wa}	와 과 놔 봐 좌
ㅐ^{ae} = ㅙ^{wae}	왜 괘 돼 쇄 홰
ㅣ^{i→e} = ㅚ^{we}	외 괴 되 쇠 회

2. Vowels created by adding other vowels to ㅜ°

Combination	Example
ㅜ°→w **+** ㅓ^{eo} = ㅝ^{weo}	워 궈 눠 둬 줘
ㅔ^e = ㅞ^{we}	웨 궤 눼 쉐 훼
ㅣⁱ = ㅟ^{wi}	위 귀 뒤 쉬 쥐

wa
와

weo
워

워라밸
WORK LIFE BALANCE

wae
왜

왜?

we
웨

노르웨이
Norway

we
외

해외
취업

wi
위

[워드코로나]
WITH COVID-19

나(와) sounds like <u>wa</u> in "<u>why</u>"

와 y

wa
나 = 工 o→w + ㅏ a

▶ TRACK 18

wa
나

ㅇ + 나 wa = 와 wa

ㄱ g + 나 wa = 과 gwa

ㅂ b + 나 wa = 봐 bwa

ㅈ j + 나 wa = 좌 jwa

ㅎ h + 나 wa = 화 hwa

^{gi} 기 ^{wa} 와 roof tile

^{gwa} 과 ^{ja} 자 snacks

^{hwa} 화 ^{ga} 가 painter

Find the letters 'consonant + ㅘ' in the images below.

과일

와인

화천

ᅫ(왜) sounds like _wae_ in "western"

왜 stern

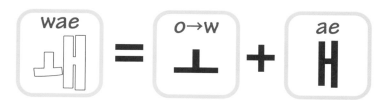

wae

ᅫ = ㅗ _o→w_ + ㅐ _ae_

▶ TRACK 19

wae
ᅫ

○ + ㅐ _wae_ = 왜 _wae_

ㄱ _g_ + ㅐ _wae_ = 괘 _gwae_

ㄷ _d_ + ㅐ _wae_ = 돼 _dwae_

ㅅ _s_ + ㅐ _wae_ = 쇄 _swae_

ㅎ _h_ + ㅐ _wae_ = 홰 _hwae_

wae
왜 ?
why?

dwae *ji*
돼 지
pig

pye *swae*
폐 쇄
shutdown

Find the letters 'consonant + ㅙ' in the images below.

돼지

폐쇄

왜가리

와 **왜** 외 워 웨 위

ㅚ(외) sounds like <u>we</u> in "wedding"

외 dding

$$ㅚ_{(we)} = ㅗ_{(o→w)} + ㅣ_{(i→e)}$$

TRACK 20

ㅚ (we)

○ + ㅚ(we) = 외(we)

ㄱ(g) + ㅚ(we) = 괴(gwe)

ㄷ(d) + ㅚ(we) = 되(dwe)

ㅅ(s) + ㅚ(we) = 쇠(swe)

ㅎ(h) + ㅚ(we) = 회(hwe)

48

외 가
_{we} _{ga}
relative on the mother's side

회 사
_{hwe} _{sa}
company

유 괴
_{yu} _{gwe}
kidnap

Find the letters 'consonant + ㅚ' in the images below.

외국어

박람회

참외

ㅝ(워) sounds like _weo_ in "worry"

워 rry

weo
ㅝ = u→w ㅜ + eo ㅓ

▶ TRACK 21

weo
ㅝ

○ + ㅝ (weo) = 워 (weo)

ㄴ (n) + ㅝ (weo) = 눠 (nweo)

ㄷ (d) + ㅝ (weo) = 둬 (dweo)

ㅁ (m) + ㅝ (weo) = 뭐 (mweo)

ㅈ (j) + ㅝ (weo) = 줘 (jweo)

sya *weo*
샤 워 shower

mweo *ye* *yo*
뭐 예 요? what's it?

jweo *yo*
쥐 요 give me st.

Find the letters 'consonant + ㅝ' in the images below.

파워

워크숍

뭐?

ㅞ(ᅰ) sounds like *we* in "*weddingern*"
ᅰddingern

we
ᅰ = *u→w* ㅜ + *e* ㅔ

▶ TRACK 22

we
ᅰ

○ + *we* ㅞ = *we* 웨

g ㄱ + *we* ㅞ = *gwe* 궤

d ㄷ + *we* ㅞ = *dwe* 뒈

s ㅅ + *we* ㅞ = *swe* 쉐

h ㅎ + *we* ㅞ = *hwe* 훼

52

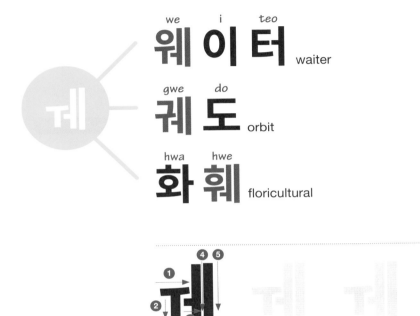

웨 *we* 이 *i* 터 *teo* waiter

궤 *gwe* 도 *do* orbit

화 *hwa* 훼 *hwe* floricultural

Find the letters 'consonant + ㅞ' in the images below.

스웨덴

스웨덴

웨딩

웨이스트

ㅟ(위) sounds like _wi_ in "we"

위

 TRACK 23

ㅟ wi

○ + ㅟ ^{wi} = 위 ^{wi}

ㄱ ^g + ㅟ ^{wi} = 귀 ^{gwi}

ㄷ ^d + ㅟ ^{wi} = 뒤 ^{dwi}

ㅅ ^s + ㅟ ^{wi} = 쉬 ^{swi}

ㅎ ^h + ㅟ ^{wi} = 휘 ^{hwi}

ga *wi*
가 위 scissors

gwi
귀 ear

dwi
뒤 back

Find the letters 'consonant + ㅟ' in the images below.

귀향

뒤집기

위기

Read and write the following words.

gi wa 기와	기와		
gwa ja 과자	과자		
hwa ga 화가	화가		
wae 왜?	왜?		
dwae ji 돼지	돼지		
pye swae 폐쇄	폐쇄		
we ga 외가	외가		
hwe sa 회사	회사		
yu gwe 유괴	유괴		

sya weo **샤워**	샤워		
mweo ye yo **뭐예요?**	뭐예요?		
jweo yo **줘요**	줘요		
we i teo **웨이터**	웨이터		
gwe do **궤도**	궤도		
hwa hwe **화훼**	화훼		
ga wi **가위**	가위		
gwi **귀**	귀		
dwi **뒤**	뒤		

4. The Diphthongs Vowel

eui		eu		i
ᅴ	=	━	+	ㅣ

▶ TRACK 24

① When '의' is the first syllable of a words, it has the pronunciation of [의](eui)

② When '의' is not the first syllable of the word, it has the pronunciation of [이](i)

③ When it is used as a possessive marker, it is pronounced as [에](e)

eui ᅴ						
	○	+	ᅴ (eui)	=	의 (eui)
	ㄴ (n)	+	ᅴ (eu)i	=	늬 (ni)
	ㅎ (h)	+	ᅴ (eu)i	=	희 (hi)
	ㄸ (dd)	+	ᅴ (eu)i	=	띄 (ddi)
	ㅆ (ss)	+	ᅴ (eu)i	=	씌 (ssi)

ᅴ(의) sounds like *eui* in "ewww"

 의www

^{eui} ^{sa}
의 사 doctor

^{ju} ⁱ
주 의 caution

^{na} ^e
나 의 my

Find the letters 'consonant + ᅴ' in the images below.

의료

파란색 꽃무늬가 있는
도자기 찻잔

꽃무늬

희망

eui sa			
의사	의사		
ju i			
주의	주의		
na e			
나의	나의		

QUIZ

▶ TRACK 25

Listen and write the words you hear.

1.

2.

3.

4.

5.

6.

7.

8.

9.

10.

What is your score?

/ 10

ANSWER

1. 아이   2. 어머니   3. 오리   4. 우주   5. 이모

6. 유리   7. 기계   8. 회사   9.가위   10. 주의

PART 2

|

Korean
Consonants

The Composition of Korean Consonants

1. The Introduction of Korean Consonants

There is a sum total of fourteen basic consonants — some of which are used twice in a conjoined format to create five double consonants. In total, you get the following 19 consonants as per the table below.

ㄱ	ㄴ	ㄷ	ㄹ	ㅁ	ㅂ	ㅅ	ㅇ	ㅈ
ㅋ		ㅌ			ㅍ		ㅎ	ㅊ
ㄲ		ㄸ			ㅃ	ㅆ		ㅉ

The following is first five basic consonants.

Adding a stroke to basic consonants such as ㄴ, ㅁ, ㅅ gives us normal-sound consonants such as ㄷ, ㅂ, ㅈ. Likewise, adding a stroke to the basic consonants such as ㄱ, ㄷ, ㅂ, ㅈ, ㅇ gives us the aspirated-sound consonant such as ㅋ, ㅌ, ㅍ, ㅊ, ㅎ.

Basic consonants and Applied consonants

Basic consonants   Applied consonants

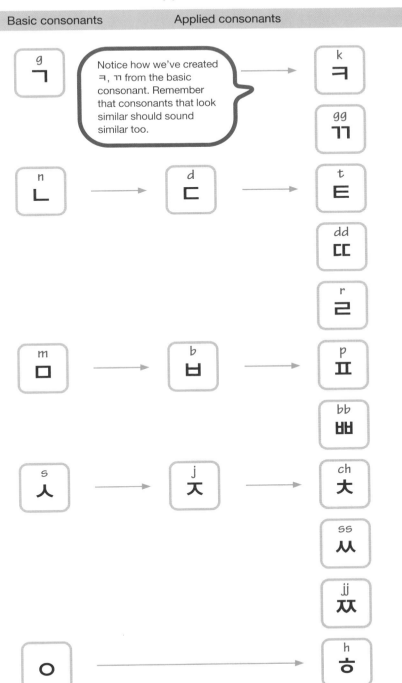

2. The Composition of Hangeul Syllables

There are three different variations to how we formulate syllables in Hangeul. First, there are stand-alone syllables with nothing but the vowel. Second, there are syllables which combine a consonant and a vowel. Third, there are syllables which put together a consonant and a vowel, joined by another consonant.

(A) Vowel Only

When a syllable is consisted of a single vowel, the empty consonant '**ㅇ**' is added to the left or above of the vowel to complete the sound.

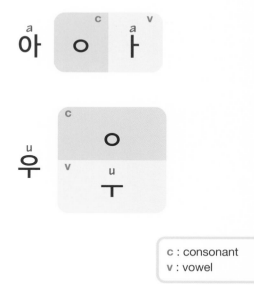

c : consonant
v : vowel

(B) Consonant + Vowel

For instance, you combine the consonant ㄴ[n] and
vowel ㅏ[a] to create 나[na]. Likewise, you combine
the consonant ㅁ[m] and vowel ㅜ[u] to create to 무[mu].

c : consonant
v : vowel

(C) Consonant + Vowel + Consonant

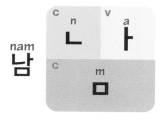

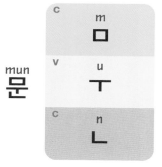

c : consonant
v : vowel

When a consonant is added underneath the consonant in a syllable, that consonant is called a 'batchim.'

Hangeul consonants are categorized into (1) Normal Sound (2) Aspirated Sound and (3) Tense Sound based on their pronunciation.

Normal sound	ㄱ	ㄴ	ㄷ	ㄹ	ㅁ	ㅂ	ㅅ	ㅇ	ㅈ
Aspirated sound	ㅋ		ㅌ			ㅍ		ㅎ	ㅊ
Tense sound	ㄲ		ㄸ			ㅃ	ㅆ		ㅉ

2

The Pronunciation of Consonants

1. Normal Sound

	ㅏ a	ㅓ eo	ㅗ o	ㅜ u	ㅐ ae	ㅔ e	ㅡ eu	ㅣ i
ㄱ g	가 ga	거 geo	고 go	구 gu	개 gae	게 ge	그 geu	기 gi
ㄴ n	나 na	너 neo	노 no	누 nu	내 nae	네 ne	느 neu	니 ni
ㄷ d	다 da	더 deo	도 do	두 du	대 dae	데 de	드 deu	디 di
ㄹ r	라 ra	러 reo	로 ro	루 ru	래 rae	레 re	르 reu	리 ri
ㅁ m	마 ma	머 meo	모 mo	무 mu	매 mae	메 me	므 meu	미 mi
ㅂ b	바 ba	버 beo	보 bo	부 bu	배 bae	베 be	브 beu	비 bi
ㅅ s	사 sa	서 seo	소 so	수 su	새 sae	세 se	스 seu	시 si
ㅇ	아 a	어 eo	오 o	우 u	애 ae	에 e	으 eu	이 i
ㅈ j	자 ja	저 jeo	조 jo	주 ju	재 jae	제 je	즈 jeu	지 ji

ㄱ (giyeok) is 'g' of gun.

g
ㄱ

ㄱ + ㅏ (*a*) = 가 (*ga*)

ㄱ + ㅓ (*eo*) = 거 (*geo*)

ㄱ + ㅗ (*o*) = 고 (*go*)

ㄱ + ㅜ (*u*) = 구 (*gu*)

ㄱ + ㅡ (*eu*) = 그 (*geu*)

ㄱ + ㅣ (*i*) = 기 (*gi*)

ㄱ + ㅐ (*ae*) = 개 (*gae*)

ㄱ + ㅔ (*e*) = 게 (*ge*)

ㄱ has the shape of a gun.
When you look at this alphabet, think of it as the letter "g" in gun.

▶ TRACK 26

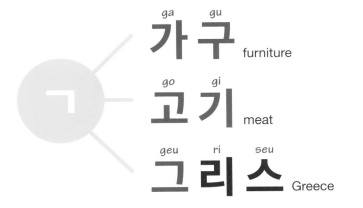

ga *gu*
가구 furniture

go *gi*
고기 meat

geu *ri* *seu*
그리스 Greece

Find the letters 'ㄱ + vowel' in the images below.

가족

군고구마, 겨울

그림

ㄱ ㄴ ㄷ ㄹ ㅁ ㅂ ㅅ ㅇ ㅈ

ㄴ (nieun) is 'n' of nose.

n
ㄴ

ㄴ + ㅏ (a) = 나 (na)

ㄴ + ㅓ (eo) = 너 (neo)

ㄴ + ㅗ (o) = 노 (no)

ㄴ + ㅜ (u) = 누 (nu)

ㄴ + ㅡ (eu) = 느 (neu)

ㄴ + ㅣ (i) = 니 (ni)

ㄴ + ㅐ (ae) = 내 (nae)

ㄴ + ㅔ (e) = 네 (ne)

ㄴ has the shape of a nose.
When you look at this alphabet, think of it as the letter "n" in nose.

누 나 — nu na — older sister

노 래 — no rae — song

나 라 — na ra — country

①

Find the letters 'ㄴ + vowel' in the images below.

나

노래

바느질

ㄷ (digeut) is 'd' of door.

d
ㄷ

ㄷ + ㅏ (a) = 다 (da)

ㄷ + ㅓ (eo) = 더 (deo)

ㄷ + ㅗ (o) = 도 (do)

ㄷ + ㅜ (u) = 두 (du)

ㄷ + ㅡ (eu) = 드 (deu)

ㄷ + ㅣ (i) = 디 (di)

ㄷ + ㅐ (ae) = 대 (dae)

ㄷ + ㅔ (e) = 데 (de)

ㄷ has the shape of a door.
When you look at this alphabet, think of it as the letter "d" in door.

▶ TRACK 28

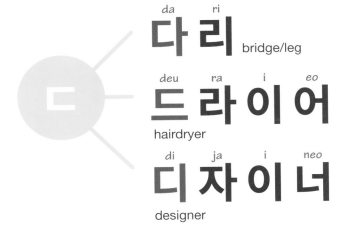

da *ri*
다 리 bridge/leg

deu *ra* *i* *eo*
드 라 이 어
hairdryer

di *ja* *i* *neo*
디 자 이 너
designer

Find the letters 'ㄷ + vowel' in the images below.

다낭

더위

제주도, 그대로

ㄱ ㄴ **ㄷ** ㄹ ㅁ ㅂ ㅅ ㅇ ㅈ

ㄹ (rieul) is 'r' of ribbon.

r
ㄹ

ㄹ + ㅏ (a) = 라 (ra)

ㄹ + ㅓ (eo) = 러 (reo)

ㄹ + ㅗ (o) = 로 (ro)

ㄹ + ㅜ (u) = 루 (ru)

ㄹ + ㅡ (eu) = 르 (reu)

ㄹ + ㅣ (i) = 리 (ri)

ㄹ + ㅐ (ae) = 래 (rae)

ㄹ + ㅔ (e) = 레 (re)

ㄹ has the shape of a ribbon.
When you look at this alphabet, think of it as the letter "r" in ribbon.

▶ **TRACK 29**

ri *deo*
리 더 leader

ra *di* *o*
라 디 오 radio

reu *po*
르 포 reportage

Find the letters 'ㄹ + vowel' in the images below.

요리

하루

모래

□ (mieum) is 'm' of mouth.

m
□

□ + ㅏ = 마
a *ma*

□ + ㅓ = 머
eo *meo*

□ + ㅗ = 모
o *mo*

□ + ㅜ = 무
u *mu*

□ + ㅡ = 므
eu *meu*

□ + ㅣ = 미
i *mi*

□ + ㅐ = 매
ae *mae*

□ + ㅔ = 메
e *me*

ㅁ has the shape of a mouth.
When you look at this alphabet, think of it as the letter "m" in mouth.

▶ **TRACK 30**

mi ni
미 니 mini

mo ja
모 자 hat

meo ri
머 리 head

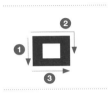

Find the letters 'ㅁ + vowel' in the images below.

메리 크리스마스

무료

매미

ㄱ ㄴ ㄷ ㄹ **ㅁ** ㅂ ㅅ ㅇ ㅈ   **79**

ㅂ (bieup) is 'b' of bucket.

b

ㅂ + ㅏ (a) = 바 (ba)

ㅂ + ㅓ (eo) = 버 (beo)

ㅂ + ㅗ (o) = 보 (bo)

ㅂ + ㅜ (u) = 부 (bu)

ㅂ + ㅡ (eu) = 브 (beu)

ㅂ + ㅣ (i) = 비 (bi)

ㅂ + ㅐ (ae) = 배 (bae)

ㅂ + ㅔ (e) = 베 (be)

ㅂ has the shape of a bucket.
When you look at this alphabet, think of it as the letter "b"
in bucket.

▶ **TRACK 31**

beo seu
버스 bus

ba da
바다 sea

bi ja
비자 visa

Find the letters 'ㅂ + vowel' in the images below.

바다

브이로그

보험, 비교

ㄱ ㄴ ㄷ ㄹ ㅁ **ㅂ** ㅅ ㅇ ㅈ

ㅅ (siot) is 's' of sandwich.

s
ㅅ

ㅅ + ㅏ (a) = 사 (sa)

ㅅ + ㅓ (eo) = 서 (seo)

ㅅ + ㅗ (o) = 소 (so)

ㅅ + ㅜ (u) = 수 (su)

ㅅ + ㅡ (eu) = 스 (seu)

ㅅ + ㅣ (i) = 시 (si)

ㅅ + ㅐ (ae) = 새 (sae)

ㅅ + ㅔ (e) = 세 (se)

ㅅ has the shape of a sandwich.
When you look at this alphabet, think of it as the letter "s" in sandwich.

seo bi seu
서 비 스 service

sa ja
사 자 lion

ga su
가 수 singer

Find the letters 'ㅅ + vowel' in the images below.

감사

서울

시간

ㅈ (jieut) is 'j' of jeans.

j
ㅈ

ㅈ + ㅏ (a) = 자 (ja)

ㅈ + ㅓ (eo) = 저 (jeo)

ㅈ + ㅗ (o) = 조 (jo)

ㅈ + ㅜ (u) = 주 (ju)

ㅈ + ㅡ (eu) = 즈 (jeu)

ㅈ + ㅣ (i) = 지 (ji)

ㅈ + ㅐ (ae) = 재 (jae)

ㅈ + ㅔ (e) = 제 (je)

ㅈ has the shape of jeans.
When you look at this alphabet, think of it as the letter "j" in jeans.

▶ **TRACK 33**

주 스 juce
ju *seu*

지 구 earth
ji *gu*

치 즈 cheese
chi *jeu*

Find the letters 'ㅈ + vowel' in the images below.

자랑, 자취

정지

주차금지

Read and write the following words.

ga gu 가구	가구		
go gi 고기	고기		
geu ri seu 그리스	그리스		
nu na 누나	누나		
no rae 노래	노래		
na ra 나라	나라		
da ri 다리	다리		
deu ra i eo 드라이어	드라이어		
di ja i neo 디자이너	디자이너		
ri deo 리더	리더		

ra di o **라디오**	라디오		
reu po **르포**	르포		
mi ni **미니**	미니		
mo ja **모자**	모자		
meo ri **머리**	머리		
beo seu **버스**	버스		
ba da **바다**	바다		
bi ja **비자**	비자		
seo bi seu **서비스**	서비스		
sa ja **사자**	사자		

ju seu 주스	주스		
ji gu 지구	지구		
chi jeu 치즈	치즈		

2. Aspirated sound

There are consonants created by adding a stroke or dot to the basic consonants 'ㄱ, ㄷ, ㅂ, ㅇ, ㅈ.'
They are 'ㅋ, ㅌ, ㅍ, ㅎ, ㅊ' and are called aspirated consonants.
When pronouncing the aspirated consonants,
please refrain from creating vibration in the vocal cord.

Aspirated Consonants: Names and Usage ⊙ TRACK 34

Consonants	Name	Pronunciation Tips	Examples
ㅋ	ki euk 키읔	Aspirated k as in kill	ka 카 ki 키 ku 쿠 ke 케 ko 코 카드 card 쿠키 cookie
ㅌ	ti eut 티읕	Aspirated t in talk	ta 타 ti 티 tu 투 te 테 to 토 타조 ostrich 도토리 acorn
ㅍ	pi eup 피읖	Aspirated p as in power	pa 파 pi 피 pu 푸 pe 페 po 포 피아노 piano 아파트 apartment
ㅎ	hi eut 히읗	Aspirated h as in how	ha 하 hi 히 hu 후 he 헤 ho 호 하나 one 오후 afternoon
ㅊ	chi eut 치읓	Aspirated ch as in change	cha 차 chi 치 chu 추 che 체 cho 초 치마 skirt 고추 chili pepper

ㅋ (kieuk) is 'k' of key.

ㅋ k

ㅋ + ㅏ a = 카 ka

ㅋ + ㅓ eo = 커 keo

ㅋ + ㅗ o = 코 ko

ㅋ + ㅜ u = 쿠 ku

ㅋ + ㅡ eu = 크 keu

ㅋ + ㅣ i = 키 ki

ㅋ + ㅐ ae = 캐 kae

ㅋ + ㅔ e = 케 ke

ㅋ has the shape of a key.
When you look at this alphabet, think of it as the letter "k" in key.

▶ **TRACK 35**

ku ki
쿠 키 cookie

ka ka o
카 카 오 cacao

ko ko a
코 코 아 cocoa

Find the letters 'ㅋ + vowel' in the images below.

스케치북

쿠키, 케이크, 마카롱

커피

ㅌ (tieut) is 't' of track.

t
ㅌ

ㅌ + ㅏ (a) = 타 (ta)

ㅌ + ㅓ (eo) = 터 (teo)

ㅌ + ㅗ (o) = 토 (to)

ㅌ + ㅜ (u) = 투 (tu)

ㅌ + ㅡ (eu) = 트 (teu)

ㅌ + ㅣ (i) = 티 (ti)

ㅌ + ㅐ (ae) = 태 (tae)

ㅌ + ㅔ (e) = 테 (te)

ㅌ has the shape of a track.
When you look at this alphabet, think of it as the letter "t" in track.

to seu teu
토 스 트 toast

gi ta
기 타 guitar

te ni seu
테 니 스 tennis

Find the letters 'ㅌ + vowel' in the images below.

토마토

투자

다이어트

ㅍ (pieup) is 'p' of piano.

p
ㅍ

ㅍ + ㅏ (a) = 파 (pa)

ㅍ + ㅓ (eo) = 퍼 (peo)

ㅍ + ㅗ (o) = 포 (po)

ㅍ + ㅜ (u) = 푸 (pu)

ㅍ + ㅡ (eu) = 프 (peu)

ㅍ + ㅣ (i) = 피 (pi)

ㅍ + ㅐ (ae) = 패 (pae)

ㅍ + ㅔ (e) = 페 (pe)

ㅍ has the shape of a piano.
When you look at this alphabet, think of it as the letter "p" in piano.

▶ TRACK 37

피 아 노 piano
pi a no

파 리 Paris
pa ri

나 이 프 knife
na i peu

Find the letters 'ㅍ + vowel' in the images below.

파티

푸시

레시피

ㅎ (hieut) is 'h' of hat.

h
ㅎ

ㅎ + ㅏ (a) = 하 (ha)

ㅎ + ㅓ (eo) = 허 (heo)

ㅎ + ㅗ (o) = 호 (ho)

ㅎ + ㅜ (u) = 후 (hu)

ㅎ + ㅡ (eu) = 흐 (heu)

ㅎ + ㅣ (i) = 히 (hi)

ㅎ + ㅐ (ae) = 해 (hae)

ㅎ + ㅔ (e) = 헤 (he)

ㅎ has the shape of a hat.
When you look at this alphabet, think of it as the letter "h" in hat.

▶ TRACK 38

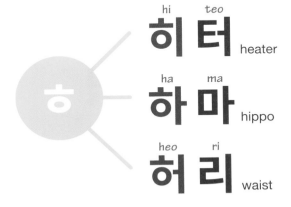

hi *teo*
히 터 heater

ha *ma*
하 마 hippo

heo *ri*
허 리 waist

Find the letters 'ㅎ + vowel' in the images below.

하나

비보호

후기

大 (chieut) is 'ch' of cha-cha-cha.

ch
大

大 + ㅏ (a) = 차 (cha)

大 + ㅓ (eo) = 처 (cheo)

大 + ㅗ (o) = 초 (cho)

大 + ㅜ (u) = 추 (chu)

大 + ㅡ (eu) = 츠 (cheu)

大 + ㅣ (i) = 치 (chi)

大 + ㅐ (ae) = 채 (chae)

大 + ㅔ (e) = 체 (che)

ㅊ has the shape of cha-cha-cha.
When you look at this alphabet, think of it as the letter "ch"
in cha-cha-cha.

▶ TRACK 39

chi *ta*
치 타 cheetah

cho
초 candle

seu *po* *cheu*
스 포 츠 sports

Find the letters 'ㅊ + vowel' in the images below.

녹차

채소

추천

Read and write the following words.

ku ki **쿠키**	쿠키		
ka ka o **카카오**	카카오		
to seu teu **토스트**	토스트		
gi ta **기타**	기타		
pi a no **피아노**	피아노		
pa ri **파리**	파리		
hi teo **히터**	히터		
heo ri **허리**	허리		
chi ta **치타**	치타		
seu po cheu **스포츠**	스포츠		

3. Tense sound

There are consonants created by conjoining two of the same consonants 'ㄱ, ㄷ, ㅂ, ㅅ, ㅈ' in order to create a set of tense-sounding consonants such as 'ㄲ, ㄸ, ㅃ, ㅆ, ㅉ' respectively. Tense sounds strain the articulators and when pronouncing these consonants, one must beware not to exhale while making the sound.

Tense Consonants: Names and Usage

🔘 **TRACK 40**

Consonants	Name	Pronunciation Tips	Examples
ㄲ	ssang gi yeok 쌍기역	Tense g as in skill	gga ggi ggu gge ggo 까 끼 꾸 께 꼬 꼬리 tail 아까 while ago
ㄸ	ssang di geut 쌍디귿	Tense d as in steel	dda ddi ddu dde ddo 따 띠 뚜 떼 또 따로 separately 이따가 later
ㅃ	ssang bi eup 쌍비읍	Tense b as in speech	bba bbi bbu bbe bbo 빠 삐 뿌 뻬 뽀 빠르다 fast 뽀뽀 kiss
ㅆ	ssang si ot 쌍시옷	Tense s as in sit	ssa ssi ssu sse sso 싸 씨 쑤 쎄 쏘 싸다 cheap 아가씨 ladies
ㅉ	ssang ji eut 쌍지읒	Tense j as in judge	jja jji jju jje jjo 짜 찌 쭈 쩨 쪼 짜다 salty 가짜 fake

ㄲ (ssang giyeok) is tense g as in skill.

gg
ㄲ

ㄲ + ㅏ (a) = 까 (gga)

ㄲ + ㅓ (eo) = 꺼 (ggeo)

ㄲ + ㅗ (o) = 꼬 (ggo)

ㄲ + ㅜ (u) = 꾸 (ggu)

ㄲ + ㅡ (eu) = 끄 (ggeu)

ㄲ + ㅣ (i) = 끼 (ggi)

ㄲ + ㅐ (ae) = 깨 (ggae)

ㄲ + ㅔ (e) = 께 (gge)

gga *chi*
까 치 magpie

ggo *ma*
꼬 마 kid

ggae
깨 sesame

ㄲ

① ㄲ ②

Find the letters 'ㄲ + vowel' in the images below.

시킬까

꾸안꾸

꼬막

ㄲ ㄸ ㅃ ㅆ ㅉ **103**

ㄸ (ssang digeut) is tense d as in steel.

dd
ㄸ

ㄸ + ㅏ *a* = 따 *dda*

ㄸ + ㅓ *eo* = 떠 *ddeo*

ㄸ + ㅗ *o* = 또 *ddo*

ㄸ + ㅜ *u* = 뚜 *ddu*

ㄸ + ㅡ *eu* = 뜨 *ddeu*

ㄸ + ㅣ *i* = 띠 *ddi*

ㄸ + ㅐ *ae* = 때 *ddae*

ㄸ + ㅔ *e* = 떼 *dde*

▶ TRACK 42

ㄸ

heo ri ddi

허 리 띠 belt

ddo

또 again

ddae ddae ro

때 때 로 sometimes

Find the letters '**ㄸ** + vowel' in the images below.

떠나자, 따라

따뜻한

뛰지

ㅃ (ssang bieup) is tense b as in speech.

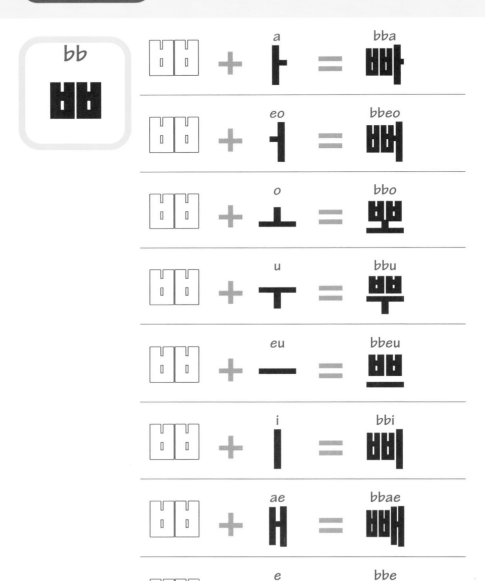

bb
ㅃ

ㅃ	+	a ㅏ	= bba 빠
ㅃ	+	eo ㅓ	= bbeo 뻐
ㅃ	+	o ㅗ	= bbo 뽀
ㅃ	+	u ㅜ	= bbu 뿌
ㅃ	+	eu ㅡ	= bbeu 쁘
ㅃ	+	i ㅣ	= bbi 삐
ㅃ	+	ae ㅐ	= bbae 빼
ㅃ	+	e ㅔ	= bbe 뻬

▶ TRACK 43

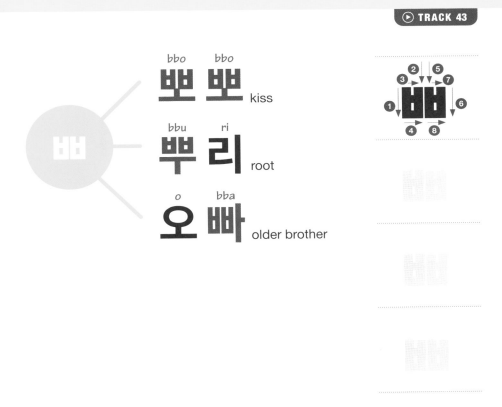

bbo   bbo
뽀 뽀 kiss

bbu   ri
뿌 리 root

o   bba
오 빠 older brother

Find the letters '**ㅃ** + vowel' in the images below.

빠른   빼빼로   뿌리

ㅆ (ssang siot) is tense s as in sit.

ss ㅆ

ㅆ + ㅏ (a) = 싸 (ssa)

ㅆ + ㅓ (eo) = 써 (sseo)

ㅆ + ㅗ (o) = 쏘 (sso)

ㅆ + ㅜ (u) = 쑤 (ssu)

ㅆ + ㅡ (eu) = 쓰 (sseu)

ㅆ + ㅣ (i) = 씨 (ssi)

ㅆ + ㅐ (ae) = 쌔 (ssae)

ㅆ + ㅔ (e) = 쎄 (sse)

ᵇⁱ ˢˢᵃ ʸᵒ
비 싸 요 expensive

ˢˢᵉᵘ ᵈᵃ
쓰 다 write

ˢˢⁱ
씨 seed

Find the letters '**ㅆ** + vowel' in the images below.

싸움

쏘가리

쓰기

ㅉ (ssang jieut) is tense j as in judge.

jj ㅉ

ㅉ + ㅏ (a) = 짜 (jja)

ㅉ + ㅓ (eo) = 쩌 (jjeo)

ㅉ + ㅗ (o) = 쪼 (jjo)

ㅉ + ㅜ (u) = 쭈 (jju)

ㅉ + ㅡ (eu) = 쯔 (jjeu)

ㅉ + ㅣ (i) = 찌 (jji)

ㅉ + ㅐ (ae) = 째 (jjae)

ㅉ + ㅔ (e) = 쩨 (jje)

ㅉ

찌 개 *jji* *gae*
Korean style stew

짜 다 *jja* *da*
salty

쪼 개 다 *jjo* *gae* *da*
spilt

Find the letters 'ㅉ + vowel' in the images below.

짜다

쪼개기

찌개

Read and write the following words.

gga chi			
까치	까치		
ggae			
깨	깨		
heo ri ddi			
허리띠	허리띠		
ddo			
또	또		
bbu ri			
뿌리	뿌리		
o bba			
오빠	오빠		
sseu da			
쓰다	쓰다		
ssi			
씨	씨		
jji gae			
찌개	찌개		
jja da			
짜다	짜다		

In Korean, a vowel and a consonant are combined to form one character, and you can further add a final consonant called **'batchim'** under the set. The batchim is an important part of Korean pronunciation because it often determines a change in the way words are pronounced.

다, 가 — no batchim

달, 갑 — ㄹ and ㅂ are the batchim

닭, 값 — ㄺ and ㅄ are the double batchim

Next, let's learn about the types of batchim and their pronunciation.

There are 16 consonants that are used as batchim, but there are only 7 kinds (ㄱ, ㄴ, ㄷ, ㄹ, ㅁ, ㅂ, ㅇ) of pronunciation.

In other words, there are different characters that have the same pronunciation.

List of batchim

ㄱ	ㄴ	ㄷ	ㄹ	ㅁ	ㅂ	ㅅ	ㅇ	ㅈ
ㅊ	ㅋ	ㅌ	ㅍ	ㅎ	ㄲ	ㅆ		

Final Consonant	How to read	Examples
ㄱ ㅋ ㄲ	ㄱ k	chaek 책(book), bu eok 부엌[부억](kitchen), bak 밖[박](outside)
ㄴ	ㄴ n	don 돈(money), san 산(mountain)
ㄷ ㅅ ㅈ ㅊ ㅌ ㅎ ㅆ	ㄷ t	sut ga rak 숟가락(spoon), ot 옷[옫](cloth), 낮[낟](noon), ggot 꽃[꼳](flower), 끝[끋](end), hi eut 히읗[히읃](the name of ㅎ), it dda 있다[읻따](being)
ㄹ	ㄹ l	dal 달(moon), 물(water) mul
ㅁ	ㅁ m	mom 몸(body), 봄(spring) bom
ㅂ ㅍ	ㅂ p	ip 입(mouth), 앞(front) ap
ㅇ	ㅇ ng	gang 강(river), 공(ball) gong

Resyllabification and Pronunciations of Korean Consonants

Suppose the previous syllable ends in a consonant in the final position, and the next syllable begins with the letter ㅇ. In that case, the consonant sound gets moved to the beginning of the following syllable.

▶ TRACK 47

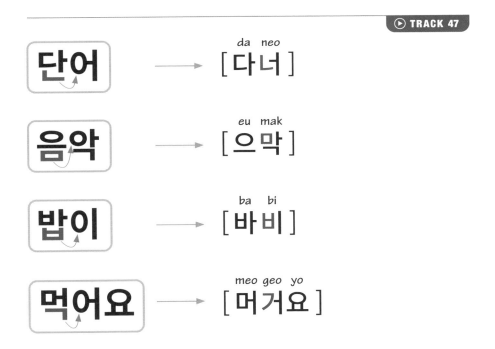

단어 ⟶ da neo [다너]

음악 ⟶ eu mak [으막]

밥이 ⟶ ba bi [바비]

먹어요 ⟶ meo geo yo [머거요]

ㄱ (ㅋ, ㄲ)

First, ㄱ, ㅋ and ㄲ make the **k** sound. These three letters look similar and can sound similar. Keep your tongue still and your throat should feel a little choked. Let's practice by reading 악, 앜, 앆.

▶ TRACK 48

Consonant		Final Consonant	
ㄱ g	**가** ga	**[ㄱ]** **k**	각[각] $^{ga}_k$
ㅋ k	**카** ka		앜[각] $^{ga}_k$
ㄲ gg	**까** gga		앆[각] $^{ga}_k$

미국 $^{gu}_k$ America

ㄱ ㅋ ㄲ

부엌 $^{eo}_k$ kitchen

밖 $^{ba}_k$ outside

Find the letters batchim [ㄱ] in the images below.

축제

팥죽, 호박죽

대한민국

ㄴ

Secondly, **ㄴ** makes the **n** sound. Your tongue should touch the back of your upper teeth. This "n" sound is the correct pronunciation of **ㄴ** batchim. Or, try slightly biting your tongue with your front teeth and say "Nnn." Let's practice this time with **안**.

▶ **TRACK 49**

Consonant		Final Consonant	
n **ㄴ**	na **나**	[ㄴ] **n**	난[난] na n

산 sa n mountain

돈 do n money

Find the letters batchim [ㄴ] in the images below.

안내

치킨

친구

ㄷ(ㅅ, ㅈ, ㅊ, ㅌ, ㅎ, ㅆ)

Consonant		Final Consonant	
ㄷ ^{d}	다 ^{da}		닫[닫] $^{da}_{t}$
ㅅ ^{s}	사 ^{sa}		삿[삳] $^{sa}_{t}$
ㅈ ^{j}	자 ^{ja}		잣[잗] $^{ja}_{t}$
ㅊ ^{ch}	차 ^{cha}	$^{[ㄷ]}$ **t**	찻[찯] $^{cha}_{t}$
ㅌ ^{t}	타 ^{ta}		탇[탇] $^{ta}_{t}$
ㅎ ^{h}	하 ^{ha}		핫[핟] $^{ha}_{t}$
ㅆ ^{ss}	싸 ^{ssa}		쌋[쌛] $^{ssa}_{t}$

ㄷ, ㅅ, ㅈ, ㅊ, ㅌ, ㅎ, ㅆ all make the t sound. The tongue should touch the back of the upper teeth. Be aware that all these 7 kinds of batchim are pronounced the same with the "t" sound. Let's try practicing 앋, 앗, 앚, 앛, 앝, 앟, 았. The batchims are different but they all have the same pronunciation.

▶ TRACK 50

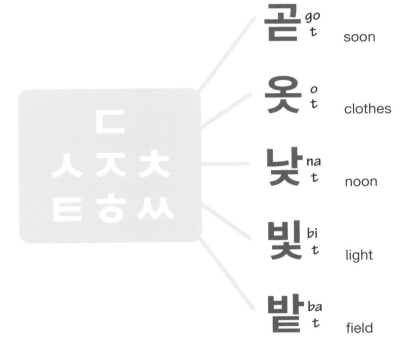

곧 *go t*	soon
옷 *o t*	clothes
낮 *na t*	noon
빛 *bi t*	light
밭 *ba t*	field

Find the letters batchim [ㄷ] in the images below.

닫아   스팟   끝

Fourthly, ㄹ makes the ㅣ sound. The tongue touches the upper teeth or the ceiling of the mouth. When you pronounce Lu, your tongue should touch the back of the ceiling of your mouth, right? This is the correct pronunciation of ㄹ. Let's practice by saying 알.

▶ TRACK 51

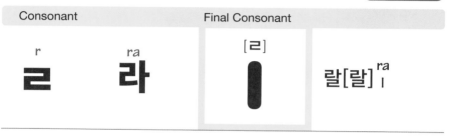

Consonant		Final Consonant	
r ㄹ	ra 라	[ㄹ] ㅣ	랄[랄] ra ㅣ

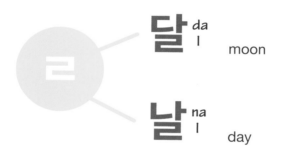

달 da
ㅣ
moon

날 na
ㅣ
day

Find the letters batchim [ㄹ] in the images below.

마늘

한달, 살기

울릉도

The fifth is **ㅁ** with the **m** sound. It's an easy pronunciation which you just need to close your mouth. Let's practice by saying **암**.

▶ TRACK 52

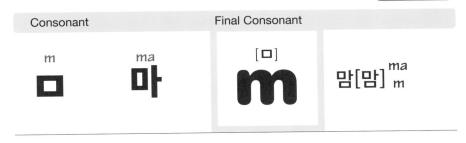

Consonant		Final Consonant	
m **ㅁ**	ma **마**	[ㅁ] **m**	맘[맘] ^{ma}_m

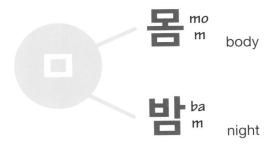

몸 ^{mo}_m body

밤 ^{ba}_m night

Find the letters batchim [ㅁ] in the images below.

봄

군밤

캠핑

ㄱ ㄲ ㅋ   ㄴ   ㄷ ㅅ ㅈ ㅊ ㅌ ㅎ ㅆ   ㄹ   ㅁ   ㅂ ㅍ   ㅇ   **121**

ㅂ and ㅍ have the **p** sound. Again, you just need to close your mouth. These also have the same pronunciation although the batchims are different. Let's practice with **압**, **앞**.

▶ **TRACK 53**

Consonant		Final Consonant	
b **ㅂ**	*ba* **바**	[ㅂ] **p**	밥[밥] *ba* *p*
p **ㅍ**	*pa* **파**		팦[팝] *pa* *p*

밥 *ba p* meal

앞 *a p* front

Find the letters batchim [ㅂ] in the images below.

국밥

집값, 매입

농업인

ㄱ ㅋ ㄲ ㄴ ㄷ ㅅ ㅈ ㅊ ㅌ ㅎ ㅆ ㄹ ㅁ **ㅂ ㅍ** ㅇ

O batchim makes the **ng** sound. When you pronounce this batchim, make a cave inside your mouth and don't move your tongue. Let's practice by saying **앙**.

▶ TRACK 54

Consonant	Final Consonant	
O	아 ᵃ	[O] **ng**

앙[앙]ᵃ ng

강 ga ng   river

공 go ng   ball

Find the letters batchim [O] in the images below.

운동, 건강   붕어빵   행복, 세상

The next is the double batchim. There are 11 double batchim in total. Some batchim are made of two consonants and they are called double batchim.

List of double batchim

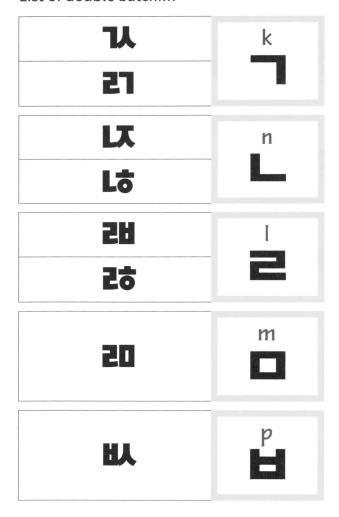

Other double batchims, such as ㄹㅅ, ㄹㅌ, and ㄹㅍ, are used less frequently and have therefore been omitted from this book.

Final Consonant	How to read	Example
ㄳ	ㄱ [k]	삯[삭] [sak] (wage)
ㄵ ㄴㅎ	ㄴ [n]	앉다[안따] [an dda] (sit) 많다[만타] [man ta] (many)
ㄺ*	ㄱ [k]	닭[닥] [dak] (chicken)
ㄼ ㄾㅎ	ㄹ [l]	여덟[여덜] [yeo deol] (eight) 잃다 [일타] [il ta] (lose)
ㄻ*	ㅁ [m]	삶[삼] [sam] (life)
ㅄ	ㅂ [p]	값[갑] [gap] (price)

* ㄺ and ㄻ are pronounced with the right consonant.

(A) Read the left batchim

ᆪ [ㄱ]	**ᆬ** [ㄴ]
삯 sa k	**앉 다** a n dda
wage	sit

ᆭ [ㄴ]	**ᆹ** [ㅂ]
많 다 ma n ta	**값** ga p
many	price

ᆲ [ㄹ]	**ᆶ** [ㄹ]
여 덟 yeo deo l	**잃 다** i l ta
eight	lose

(B) Read the right batchim

ᆰ [ᄀ]^k	ᆱ [ᄆ]^m
닭 da k	삶 sa m
chicken	life

* The letters ᆰ and ᆱ are read on the right.

Find the letters **double batchim** in the images below.

끓여서   닭   많이

In some cases, when the next syllable begins with a vowel,
the sound of the latter of the consonants simply gets transferred
to the following syllable.

값 ⟶ [갑]
gap

값이 ⟶ [갑시]
gap si

닭 ⟶ [닥]
dak

닭이 ⟶ [달기]
dal gi

삶 ⟶ [삼]
sam

삶이 ⟶ [살미]
sal mi

Read and write the following words.

mi guk 미국	미국		
bu eok 부엌	부엌		
bak 밖	밖		
san 산	산		
don 돈	돈		
got 곧	곧		
ot 옷	옷		
nat 낮	낮		
bit 빛	빛		
bat 밭	밭		

dal 달	달		
nal 날	날		
mom 몸	몸		
bam 밤	밤		
bap 밥	밥		
ap 앞	앞		
gang 강	강		
gong 공	공		

sak 삯	삯		
an dda 앉다	앉다		
man ta 많다	많다		
dak 닭	닭		
yeo deol 여덟	여덟		
il ta 잃다	잃다		
sam 삶	삶		
gap 값	값		

APPENDIX

1. Various fonts in Hangeul

가 나 다 라 마 바 사

아 자 차 카 타 파 하

가 나 다 라 마 바 사

아 자 차 카 타 파 하

가 나 다 라 마 바 사

아 자 차 카 타 파 하

가 나 다 라 마 바 사

아 자 차 카 타 파 하

2. Korean basic expression

▶ TRACK 58

an-nyeong
안녕!

Hi!

안녕!

▶ TRACK 59

an-nyeong-ha-se-yo
안녕하세요.

Hello.

안녕하세요.

ban-ga-weo-yo
반가워요.

Nice to meet you.

반가워요.

cheo-eum bwep-get-sseum-ni-da
처음 뵙겠습니다.

It's a pleasure to meet you.

처음 뵙겠습니다.

o-raen-ma-ni-e-yo
오랜만이에요.

오랜만이에요.

Long time no see.

jal   ji-naet-sseo-yo
잘 지냈어요?

잘 지냈어요?

Have you been well?

an-nyeong-hi　gye-se-yo
안녕히 계세요.

Bye. (The one sending sb off)

안녕히 계세요.

an-nyeong-hi　ga-se-yo
안녕히 가세요.

Bye. (The one leaving sb)

안녕히 가세요.

ne
네.

네.

Yes.

a-ni-yo
아니요.

아니요.

No.

go-ma-weo-yo

고마워요.

Thank you.

고마워요.

gam-sa-ham-ni-da

감사합니다.

Thank you.

감사합니다.

cheon-ma-ne-yo
천만에요.

천만에요.

You're welcome.

sil-le-ham-ni-da
실례합니다.

실례합니다.

Excuse me.

mi-an-hae-yo
미안해요.

미안해요.

Sorry.

gwaen-cha-na-yo
괜찮아요.

괜찮아요.

It's okay.

il 일 1	일		i 이 2	이
sam 삼 3	삼		sa 사 4	사
o 오 5	오		yuk 육 6	육
chil 칠 7	칠		pal 팔 8	팔
gu 구 9	구		sip 십 10	십

ha-na		dul	
하나 1	하나	둘 2	둘

set		net	
셋 3	셋	넷 4	넷

da-seot		yeo-seot	
다섯 5	다섯	여섯 6	여섯

il-gop		yeo-deol	
일곱 7	일곱	여덟 8	여덟

a-hop		yeol	
아홉 9	아홉	열 10	열